STORMS--

FROM THE INSIDE OUT

Books by Malcom E. Weiss

Storms—From The Inside Out
Man Explores The Sea
Clues To The Riddle of Life

STORMS--
FROM THE INSIDE OUT

by Malcolm E. Weiss

ILLUSTRATED BY LLOYD BIRMINGHAM
and with photographs

JULIAN MESSNER NEW YORK

Published by Julian Messner, a Division of Simon & Schuster, Inc.
1 West 39 Street, New York, N. Y. 10018. All rights reserved.

Map on page 79 © 1969 by The New York Times Company.
Reprinted by permission.

Picture Credits
Lloyd Birmingham: p. 12-13, 18, 19, 34, 39, 47, 51, 58, 61,
   64, 65, 66, 70
National Center for Atmospheric Research (NCAR): p. 30, 40-41
National Oceanic and Atmospheric Administration (NOAA): p. 15, 28-29,
   32-33, 45, 57, 68, 69, 71
The New York Public Library Picture Collection: p. 11
The New York Times: p. 79
Joan Schuman Photo: p. 77
Malcolm E. Weiss: p. 22-23

Printed in the United States of America

Library of Congress Cataloging in Publication Data

Weiss, Malcom E.
   Storms—from the inside out.

   SUMMARY: Discusses the atmospheric conditions which
result in hurricanes, tornadoes, cyclones, thunder,
lightning, and clouds.
   1. Storms—Juvenile literature. [1. Storms.
2. Weather] I. Birmingham, Lloyd, illus. II. Title.
QC941.3.W44   551.5'5   73-5396
ISBN 0-671-32611-2
ISBN 0-671-32612-0 (lib. bdg.)

For Ann
in every kind of weather

Contents

chapter

1. The Admiral Gets A Weather Eye 9

2. Clouds—Weather Made Visible 17

3. Clouds That Explore 26

4. Lightning! 36

5. Deadly Funnel 44

6. Hurricane! 54

7. The Biggest Storms 63

8. Scientific Guessing 75

Safety Rules 83

Glossary 89

Index 91

chapter **1**

The Admiral Gets a Weather Eye

"In all the Indies, I have always found the weather like May," Christopher Columbus wrote happily to friends in Spain.

Columbus—Admiral of the Ocean Sea—had good reason to be happy. His three small ships, the Niña, the Pinta, and the Santa María, had crossed the Atlantic Ocean safely.

On October 12, 1492, Columbus landed on San Salvador Island in the Caribbean Sea. As the year came to a close, he sailed his ships along the coast of what is now Cuba.

According to the calendar, it was winter, but the weather was like May. The days were warm and sunny, and the nights were bright with stars. The wind blew steadily, filling the ships'

sails and raising small waves. But it never blew
hard enough to endanger the ships. Most of that
winter, Columbus sailed the Caribbean without
dropping anchor.

Columbus did not know how lucky he
was. The Caribbean Sea has some of the world's
worst weather, especially in the fall and early
winter. Hurricanes with winds of over 100 miles
an hour and violent thunderstorms are common.

Columbus made three more voyages to this
part of the world. Each time, he learned more
about the weather of the Caribbean. By 1502, the
year of his fourth and last voyage, he knew bet-
ter than to trust the sunny skies of the Indies.

In June of that year, Columbus sailed his
four ships into the harbor of Santo Domingo. He
sent one of his captains ashore to talk to the governor of Hispaniola—and to convey a warning.

The warning was that a hurricane was coming. In the harbor were 30 ships, loaded with
treasure to be taken back to Spain. Columbus
warned the governor not to let the ships sail until
the storm passed. He also asked permission to
shelter his own ships at Santo Domingo.

The haughty governor ignored the warning
and refused the plea. Secure in his knowledge of
the weather, Columbus sailed his ships ten miles

10

On his fourth voyage, Columbus faced stormy seas in the Caribbean.

west to another harbor. The governor's fleet turned eastward toward the open ocean and Spain.

Within two days, a hurricane struck the area in full force. Safe in harbor, Columbus' ships rode out the storm. Most of the governor's ships sank with all hands aboard. Only one of his ships made it to Spain—a ship carrying gold belonging to Columbus.

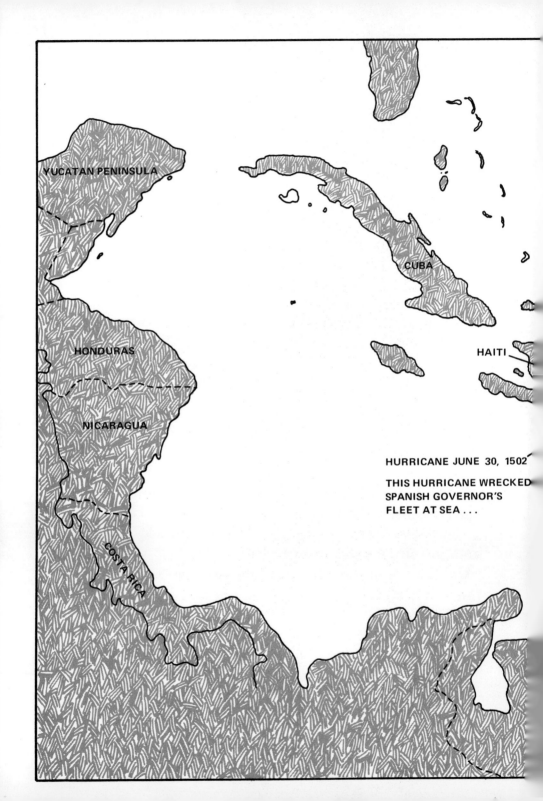

YUCATAN PENINSULA

CUBA

HONDURAS

HAITI

NICARAGUA

COSTA RICA

HURRICANE JUNE 30, 1502

THIS HURRICANE WRECKED
SPANISH GOVERNOR'S
FLEET AT SEA . . .

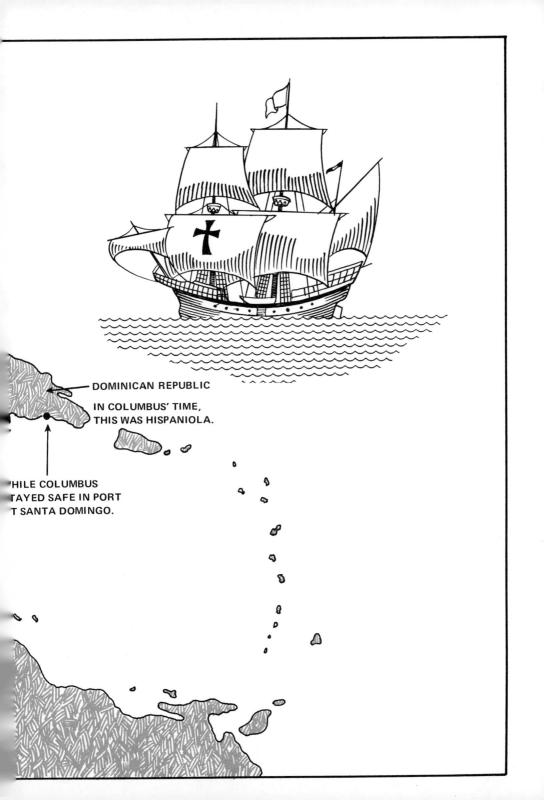

DOMINICAN REPUBLIC

IN COLUMBUS' TIME,
THIS WAS HISPANIOLA.

...HILE COLUMBUS
...TAYED SAFE IN PORT
...T SANTA DOMINGO.

The admiral's friends were delighted. But his enemies in Spain whispered that it was all done by black magic and witchcraft.

The truth is simple. That one ship may have escaped by luck. But Columbus, who could no more control the winds than could the governor of Hispaniola, knew how to read their message. He had spent four voyages learning from the clouds and the sea, and the shifting winds that billowed out the sails of his ships.

As he sailed into Santo Domingo, Columbus saw the thin haze over the sky. He saw high, feathery clouds flying with great speed through the air, and the long, heavy waves building up from the southeast. All these signs told him that somewhere, not far off, a hurricane was moving over the ocean—in the direction of the harbor. Columbus understood the signs, and acted on them.

Today, weather satellites circle the Earth, taking pictures of cloud and storm patterns all over the world. Violent storms are tracked from space, and ships or cities in their path receive plenty of advance warning.

Keeping track of the storms in the United States alone is a full-time job for some of these satellites. Perhaps nowhere else in the world do storms vary as much in strength and size as they

An approaching hurricane stirs up huge waves.

do in this country. They vary from the gentlest summer shower to the savage tornado that can tear a trailer truck apart and wrap its remains around a tree trunk.

And tornadoes, destructive as they are, are small indeed compared with the giant winter storms that cross the country. A tornado is so small that it can wreck a farmhouse on one side of the road and leave a building on the other side unharmed. It is so short-lived that it may vanish within ten minutes. Winter storms, on the other hand, can affect the weather over half the country at one time.

But, like Columbus, you do not need complicated instruments to understand storms and their ways wherever you live. The stories of storms past and storms yet to come are written across the sky —if you know how to read the words.

The words are the restless, changing shapes of the clouds themselves.

chapter 2

Clouds—Weather
Made Visible

What are clouds? You don't have to fly through one in a plane to find out. You can see clouds in your kitchen every day!

The whitish smoky-looking stuff coming out of the spout of a teakettle of boiling water is a cloud. You can find out what this cloud is made of by holding a pie plate in the cloud.

The plate will quickly become covered with many tiny drops of water. That's what the teakettle cloud and practically all clouds in the sky are made of—huge numbers of water droplets floating in the air. What's more, the cloud over the teakettle forms in exactly the same way that clouds form in the sky.

Look closely at the spout of the teakettle. You'll see that the cloud doesn't form at the spout, but a little above it. In between the cloud and the spout is a small clear space. Here, heated air is rising up from the spout.

A "cloud" of steam and a cumulus cloud form in much the same way. In each case, heated air containing invisible water vapor rises. As it rises, it cools. The water vapor condenses into millions of tiny water droplets, forming a cloud.

INVISIBLE WATER VAPOR

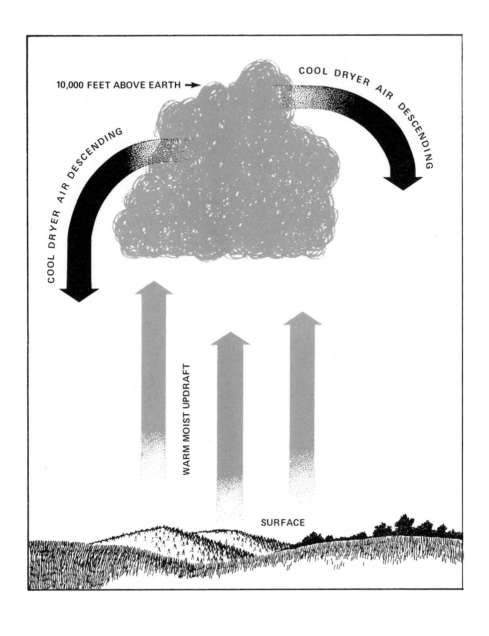

This heated air has lots of water in it, but you can't see the water. That's because it is in the form of invisible gas—water vapor. The water vapor comes from the water in the kettle.

A short distance above the spout, some of the water vapor condenses—it turns back into water again. The water droplets that form make a visible cloud.

As the water vapor condenses, it gives off heat energy. This energy was stored in the water vapor. Let's see what this means.

It takes heat to turn the water in the kettle into water vapor. When the water vapor condenses back into water, this heat is given off again. This happens whenever water vapor condenses. In later chapters, we will see how this released heat energy helps make storms.

Why does the water vapor condense? It does so because the air cools as it moves away from the hot teakettle. The cooler the air, the less water vapor it can hold. So a cloud forms above the spout. This cloud tells a story—that warm moist air is rising from the spout and cooling.

The small, fluffy white clouds that you see in the sky on a sunny summer day are formed in the same way. On such days, the summer sun heats up the ground quickly. The ground heats the air next to it. Because warm air is lighter than cold air, this sun-warmed air begins to rise. It forms a rising column of air like an invisible fountain. This rising air is called an updraft.

The updraft contains water vapor. In fact, air always contains some water vapor. This water vapor comes from damp ground, plants, rivers, and oceans. Water from the surface of these things turns into water vapor — eVAPORates — even at ordinary temperatures. That's what happens to the water in clothes left out to dry.

As the updraft rises and moves away from the hot ground, it cools. When it rises high enough and becomes cool enough, water droplets condense in the updraft. Millions of these droplets floating together make up one of the fluffy clouds so common in fair-weather summer skies.

Meteorologists — scientists who study the weather—call such clouds cumulus clouds, from a Latin word meaning to heap up. Often, such clouds do look like piled-up heaps of cotton.

These clouds make certain changes in the air visible. They show where updrafts are rising into the sky and cooling. And wherever storms

Cumulus clouds
float over Raccoon
Cove, near Mt.
Desert Island,
Maine.

are being born, clouds form, too. They tell the story of changing conditions in the air that make the storm.

Storms form only in the lower part of the atmosphere—the envelope of gases that surrounds our world. Above a height of seven miles or so, there are no storms.

There's a good reason for this. All storms consist of air in motion. In thunderstorms, the air is in violent vertical (up-and-down) motion. In other storms, such as tornadoes, hurricanes, and the huge storms of winter, the air swirls about the storm center.

We've already seen one example of air in motion—the updraft. The air in an updraft rises because it has become warmer than the surrounding air. Such temperature differences are necessary to start air moving.

In the lower atmosphere, the temperature drops steadily with increasing height. It drops about seven degrees fahrenheit for every 2,000-foot rise.

At seven miles up, the temperature drops to an icy 67 degrees below zero—and stops falling. From seven to 12 miles up, there are no temperature differences and no storms. Above 12 miles, there is too little air for any kind of weather.

24

Scientists call the lower, stormy part of the atmosphere the troposphere, meaning the sphere of changes. It is a place of sudden and dramatic changes made visible by clouds.

It is a place where cumulus clouds (plural: cumuli) explode.

chapter 3

Clouds That Explode

Why do some cumulus clouds explode? To find the answers, let's follow the birth and growth of a cloud that explodes.

It's late morning on a hot August day. For several hours, the sun has been heating up the ground. The ground, in turn, heats up the air next to it. Warm, moist updrafts form. The updrafts rise and cool, and soon there are cumulus clouds across the sky in great number.

At first, the air above these clouds is dry. As the cloud tops poke their way into this dry air, the water droplets that make up the clouds quickly evaporate. The clouds do not grow very much, if at all. The dry air acts like a "ceiling" above them. The droplets hitting the ceiling evaporate at just about the same rate that new water droplets condense from the cooling updraft beneath them.

The updraft is now cooler, and hence heavier than the air about it. It begins to sink back toward the ground as a <u>downdraft</u>. At ground level, the air picks up still more heat and moisture from the sun-warmed land. As warm, moist air, it becomes part of the updraft column once again, carrying heat and moisture from the ground up to cloud level.

The clouds tell the story. The cumulus clouds mark the tops of updrafts. The spaces of open sky mark areas where cool, dry air is returning to the ground.

But as the hours pass, the clouds begin to tell a different story. Updrafts feed more and more water vapor into the air above the cloud tops. At last, some of this air becomes <u>saturated</u>. It has absorbed all the water vapor it can hold. This saturated air no longer acts like a ceiling. No more water droplets evaporate into the saturated air. So the water droplets pile up at the cloud tops. Now the clouds begin to grow and billow upward. They seem to explode.

A cumulus cloud
begins "exploding"
upward through
saturated air....

As the top of an exploding cloud surges upward, it changes. The upper edge becomes fuzzy, flattens, and spreads out. Why? Because it has reached the top of the troposphere.

When the top of the cloud breaks through the troposphere, it can rise no higher. It flattens out into the familiar anvil shape of a thunderhead. In the bitter cold, water droplets freeze into snow and ice crystals.

The snow and ice crystals in the cloud top grow heavier, and they fall through the cloud. In falling, they drag large amounts of air with them. As the air sinks, the ice in it melts. This melting cools the surrounding air. In much the same way, melting ice cubes cool a drink.

By the time the falling air hits the earth's surface, the air is quite cool. That's why you often feel a chilly gust of wind just as a thunderstorm passes overhead.

Just before it does, everything is dark, still, hot, and damp. Thunder rumbles distantly. Then there is that surprising gust of cold air.

Things are no longer still. Leaves rustle,

Its top begins to spread out as it hits the "ceiling" of the troposphere ....

And finally
it becomes a
full-fledged
cumulonimbus
or thunderstorm
cloud.

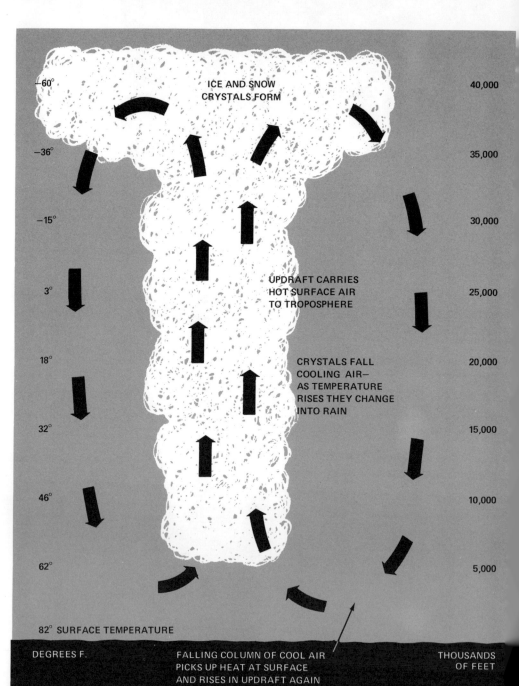

ICE AND SNOW
CRYSTALS FORM

UPDRAFT CARRIES
HOT SURFACE AIR
TO TROPOSPHERE

CRYSTALS FALL
COOLING AIR—
AS TEMPERATURE
RISES THEY CHANGE
INTO RAIN

−60°   40,000

−36°   35,000

−15°   30,000

3°   25,000

18°   20,000

32°   15,000

46°   10,000

62°   5,000

82° SURFACE TEMPERATURE

DEGREES F.   FALLING COLUMN OF COOL AIR   THOUSANDS
                  PICKS UP HEAT AT SURFACE   OF FEET
                  AND RISES IN UPDRAFT AGAIN

branches creak, washing flaps on the line, and doors slam. Suddenly, the rain comes down in torrents. Lightining flashes, making the clouds glow from within. The thunder's rumbles grow to a roar—with many echoes, like giant drums played out of step. A full-fledged thunderstorm is under way.

As this diagram shows, a thunderstorm often helps to even out differences between high air temperatures near the ground and cooler air temperatures at greater heights. Hot air at the surface rises and cools. Water condensing out of the air turns into ice and snow. The ice and snow fall toward the ground and cool the air as they pass through it.

chapter 4

Lightning!

For most Americans, the Fourth of July means a long summer weekend. But for a few each year, the holiday means death or injury—from lightning.

During one such weekend, two men were injured by lightning on a golf course in Greenfield, Indiana. On another golf course, in West Virginia, lightning seriously hurt a boy carrying golf clubs, and set buildings on a hilltop afire. Another boy, who took shelter under a tree, was killed when the tree was struck.

On that July weekend, eight persons in 18 states were injured and two were killed by lightning. Some five million dollars' worth of damage was done.

What is lightning? It is a gigantic spark of electricity. Except in size and power, it is no different from the feeble spark you get when you shuffle across a carpet on a dry day and then bring a finger very close to a metal door knob.

Both the giant spark of lightning and the small spark that leaps from your finger are caused by friction — rubbing together. Your shoes rubbing against the carpet help make the small spark. In thunderstorms, the amount of friction and the electricity produced by the friction are far greater. Water droplets and ice, snow, and dust particles rub together as they swirl in the strong winds.

In your body and in the storm cloud, friction causes charges of electricity to build up. There are two kinds of charges. One kind is called positive; the other, negative.

Charges that are alike repel each other. In other words, positive charges tend to move away from other nearby positive charges. Negative charges also repel each other.

Unlike charges, however, attract each other. Negative and positive charges tend to move toward each other.

Where do these charges come from? They are built right into the atoms that make up your shoes, the carpet, the particles in the storm clouds, and everything else in the universe. Each atom has a nucleus, which contains positive charges called protons. Around the nucleus swirl negative charges called electrons.

In the normal atom, the number of swirling electrons equals the number of protons in the nucleus. The opposite charges cancel each other out. So the atom behaves as if it had no charge at all.

But this can easily be changed. Electrons on the outer "edge" of some atoms can be moved by rubbing. You see the results of this sometimes when you run a hard rubber comb through your hair. Sparks crackle. Your hair stands up as if pulled by some mysterious invisible force in the comb.

What's going on? Friction causes some electrons from the atoms making up your hair to move into the comb. Now the comb has extra electrons. So it has a negative charge. Your hair, though, has fewer electrons than protons. So your hair has a positive charge. Since unlike charges attract, the comb and your hair attract each other.

In much the same way, but on a far larger scale, friction builds up electrical charges in a thunderstorm. As a rule, positive charges build up at the top of the cloud while negative charges build up at the bottom.

As the thunderstorm passes over the ground, the negative charge on the bottom of the cloud

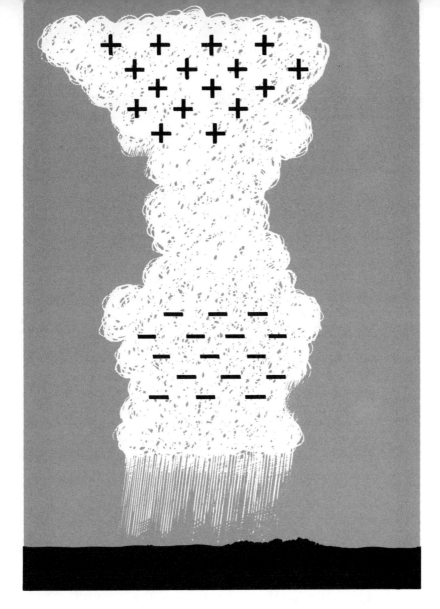

Usually positive charges are at the top of a thunderstorm cloud, while negative charges collect at the bottom.

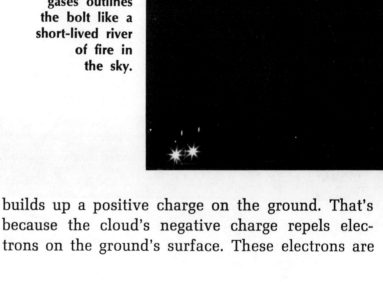

An electrical "spark" three miles long, this lightning bolt strikes southeast of Boulder, Colorado. Each fork and branch of the spark marks the path of electrical charges hurtling between cloud and ground. The moving charges heat the air nearby intensely. The flash of white-hot gases outlines the bolt like a short-lived river of fire in the sky.

builds up a positive charge on the ground. That's because the cloud's negative charge repels electrons on the ground's surface. These electrons are

40

driven beneath the surface. Now the surface has an excess of protons and thus a positive charge.
    In a full-fledged thunderstorm, huge elec-

trical charges build up within the cloud and on the ground beneath it in a matter of seconds. The attraction between opposite charges grows stronger and stronger. Finally, a bolt of lightning spears through the cloud, or hurtles between cloud and ground.

What path will the lightning bolt follow? Lightning usually follows the shortest path between cloud and objects on the ground. For this reason, lightning often strikes tall buildings, trees standing alone in a field, and other high objects.

If the building has a steel frame, the lightning does it no harm. Nor does it harm the people in the building. That's because steel, like most metals, is a good conductor of electricity. In other words, electricity flows through it easily.

In effect, a building with a steel frame is what is called a Faraday cage. In 1836, British scientist Michael Faraday built the first Faraday cage, a 12-foot metal-lined box. He showed that the space outside the box could have electric sparks flashing everywhere—yet no electricity ever got inside the box. Thus, such a building protects people in it from the hurtling threat of lightning.

And "hurtles" is just the right word. Charges in a lightning bolt may travel at speeds up to 93,000 miles a second! These charges also heat up the air they pass through. Air temperature in a lightning bolt may reach 54,000 degrees Fahrenheit. This tremendous heat causes the air to move outward from the lightning bolt in all directions.

This violent outward motion of the heated air is called a shock wave. A fast-flying jet plane makes a similar shock wave as it pushes the air in its path out of the way. The jet shock wave causes the booming sound of jet flight. The shock wave produced by lightning causes thunder.

So the thunder always comes after the lightning. The thunder may be a frightening sound, but if you can hear it, you know you're safe.

In fact, thunder is just the "big brother" of that crackling noise you hear when a spark leaps from your hand to the door knob. That small spark heats the air, too. But the amount of heat is much less than that in a lightning bolt. So the sound is a crackle instead of a roar.

It was Benjamin Franklin, over 200 years ago, who first saw that the spark's crackle was like the boom of thunder. After all, said Franklin, if a tiny spark can make a loud snap, "how loud must be the crack of 10,000 acres of electrified cloud?"

chapter 5

Deadly Funnel

In one out of a hundred thunderstorms, a whirling, twisting roaring funnel grows downward from the base of the storm. The funnel touches the ground and turns black as dust and dirt are sucked up. A tornado—the most violent storm on earth—has been born. Few people have looked into the heart of a tornado and lived to talk about it. One who did was Kansas farmer Will Keller.

On the afternoon of a hot, muggy June day, Keller was out in his field when he looked up and saw a tornado bearing down on him. He ran to his tornado cellar, which he had built underground with a strong overhead door. He had also made sure there was an air outlet. Such a shelter provides the only complete protection against tornadoes.

Keller was about to close the door when he turned around for a last look at the tornado. He noticed that the whirling lower end of the funnel-shaped cloud was beginning to rise off the ground. He knew that as long as the funnel was not touching the ground, he would be safe, even if it passed directly overhead. And if it did start down, he could dive into the cellar and shut the door quickly. As he watched at the edge of the cellar, he was fascinated by what he saw. This is his description:

"Steadily the tornado came on, the end gradually rising above the ground. I could have stood there only a few seconds, but so impressed was I with what was going on that it seemed like a long time.

"At last the great shaggy end of the funnel hung directly overhead. Everything was as still as death. There was a strong gassy odor, and it seemed I could not breathe. There was a screaming, hissing sound coming directly from the end of the funnel. I looked up, and to my astonishment I saw right into the heart of the tornado.

"There was a circular opening in the center of the funnel, about 50 or 100 feet in diameter, extending straight upward for a distance of at least one-half mile, as best I could judge. . . . The

This is how one eyewitness described the appearance of a tornado. ➡

walls of this opening were of rotating clouds . . . made brilliantly visible by constant flashes of lightning which zigzagged from side to side. Had it not been for the lightning, I could not have seen the opening. . . ."

Mr. Keller was lucky to reach his cellar in time. Hundreds of people are killed each year by tornadoes, and thousands more are injured. Damage is over a billion dollars. Much of this destruction is caused by the terrible speed of the winds

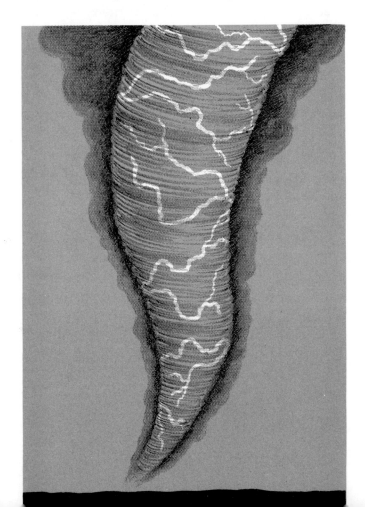

swirling around the tornado's center. No one has ever measured the speed of these winds because there are no wind-speed instruments strong enough to survive in a tornado.

However, scientists can judge the speed of a tornado's winds indirectly, by noting what the winds do to objects in their path. From such evidence, scientists estimate that the wind speed ranges from a low of about 200 miles an hour to a high of 600 miles an hour or even higher. Here are some examples of the tornado's awesome power:

Tornado winds tore five 70-ton railroad coaches from their tracks. One coach was blown a distance of 80 feet and dropped into a ditch. The spire of a church was carried 15 miles through the air. A house was carried two miles. Lengths of lumber were driven through buildings and tree trunks as though they were spears. Huge trees were twisted around and snapped off at their roots.

Forces other than damaging winds are also at work inside tornadoes. Sometimes, as the writhing, twisting funnel passes over a house, the house seems to explode. The walls and ceiling burst apart as if a bomb had gone off inside. In fact, this is a real explosion. Its cause is the low air pressure at the center of the tornado.

The pressure at the center of a tornado may be only 13 pounds per square inch. However, inside the house, the air pressure is normal, about 15 pounds per square inch. The difference of two pounds per square inch between inside and outside pressure may not seem like much. But stop and think about it.

Suppose a tornado funnel passes over a small building that measures 20 by 10 by 10 feet. On each square inch of the building, there is two pounds of pressure from the inside that is not balanced by air pressure outside the building. On the ceiling, that adds up to an unbalanced pressure of 57,600 pounds. The pressure on the four walls adds up to 288,000 pounds.

If windows are open in the building, some of the inside air will simply rush out through them. This will balance the pressure inside and outside the building. But if windows are shut tight, the enormous inside pressure may cause the building to burst apart.

Unfortunately, heavy rain and hail often occur in thunderstorms that later produce tornadoes. So people frequently shut all windows to protect their property. This may cause far worse damage later. For the same reason, tornado cellars must have an air vent. Otherwise, the cellar door might be blown out when a tornado passes over it.

The number of tornadoes in the United States averages about 642 a year. Most of them form during the late spring and early summer in the Great Plains states, from the Gulf of Mexico to the Canadian border. In fact, tornadoes strike so frequently in Texas, Oklahoma, Kansas, Nebraska, and Iowa that this area is sometimes called "tornado alley."

These states have more tornadoes than any other place in the world. This is because in spring and summer, two very different kinds of air meet over the Great Plains.

As cold air moves down from the Western mountains, it passes over mile after mile of sun-baked land. This air becomes very hot and dry near the Earth's surface. But higher up, the air is very cold—as cold as the mountaintops from which it came. The air moves rapidly over the Great Plains, where there are few mountains or hills to slow it down.

Warm, very moist air from the Gulf lies over the ground. Above the moist air is a thin layer of warm dry air. Above that is a layer of very cold air. The stage is set for violent thunderstorms and, possibly, tornadoes.

This is how hailstones form in some severe thunderstorms. ➤

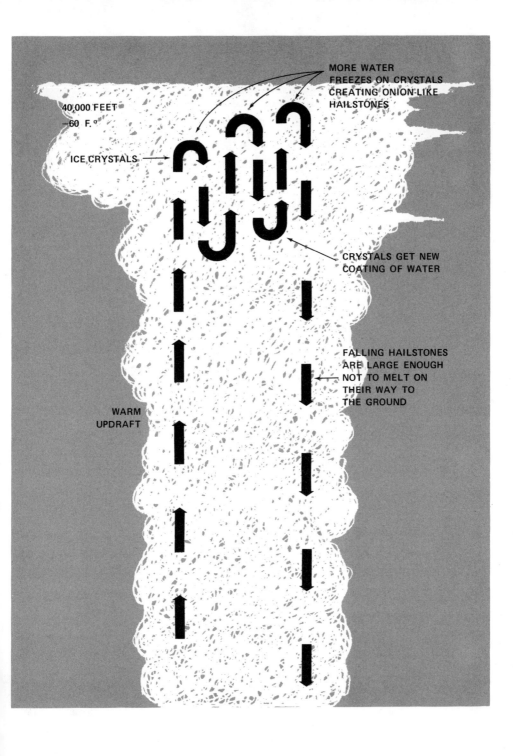

Just a slight change in these conditions will release enormous amounts of heat energy, which is stored in the water vapor in the moist air.

This moist air lies near the ground. During the afternoon, it picks up heat from the sun-warmed Earth. By late afternoon, it is warmer and lighter than the thin dry layer above it. The moist air rises through that layer and breaks into the cold air above. Almost instantly, tons of water vapor start condensing out of the moist air. The heat that is released causes strong updrafts.

The updrafts in these storms are so powerful that the storms produce large amounts of hail. Air moving into the storm begins to swirl around the updraft. That's because the Earth's spin causes air to swirl as it moves over the Earth's surface.

In spring and summer, giant thunderstorms with swirling winds form day after day in tornado alley. In perhaps one out of a hundred storms, the swirling winds move downward from the base of a thunderstorm—and a tornado strikes.

Scientists still do not know quite why this happens. But they have discovered that when warm, moist air from the Gulf of Mexico collides with dryer air from the mountains, tornadoes are possible. At hundreds of weather stations across the Great Plains, meteorologists are on the alert for such a collision. Wherever it occurs, the scientists issue a <u>tornado watch.</u>

This warns people to keep tuned to radio or TV stations for further news. It also alerts volunteers in the tornado watch area to be on the lookout for tornadoes. As soon as one is sighted, the volunteer calls the nearest weather station, which issues a <u>tornado warning.</u> People in the area should be ready to take shelter immediately, even if the sky seems clear. This tornado alert network—called SKYWARN—has saved hundreds of lives each year in the Great Plains states.

In 1973, SKYWARN got a real workout. For some reason, warm moist air from the Gulf of Mexico moved northward over the Great Plains for most of the year. There were more tornadoes in the U.S. than the Weather Service had ever recorded—over 1,100 of them. In one four-day period at the end of May, 190 tornadoes tore through Tornado Alley.

Dr. George P. Cressman, Director of the National Weather Service, said: "It used to be that for every two tornadoes reported, about three lives were lost. On that basis, over 1,700 lives should have been lost this year, with perhaps five times as many people injured. Yet less than 100 lives were lost. The warning system . . . saved 1,600 lives."

chapter 6

Hurricane!

Eight hundred miles above the Caribbean Sea, a weather satellite orbits the earth. Automatic television cameras click busily, photographing the scene below. It is a view that Columbus could not have hoped for in his wildest dreams.

For the most part, the view is cloudless. But some 300 miles north of Puerto Rico, a coil of clouds seems to hang motionless in the air. Within that 100-mile-wide coil, winds are swirling faster and faster. A hurricane is forming.

Hurricanes get their start over the warm tropical waters of the North Atlantic Ocean near the equator. Most hurricanes appear in late summer or early fall, when sea temperatures are at their highest. The warm water heats the air above it, and updrafts of warm, moist air begin rising.

Day after day, fluffy cumuli form atop the updrafts. But the cloud tops rarely rise higher than about 6,000 feet.

At that height in the tropics, there is usually a layer of warm, dry air that acts like an invisible ceiling or lid.

Once in a while, something happens in the upper air that destroys this lid. Scientists don't know yet quite how this happens. But when it does, it's the first step in the birth of a hurricane.

With the lid off, the warm, moist air rises higher and higher. Heat energy, released as the water vapor in the air condenses, drives the updrafts to heights of 50,000 to 60,000 feet. The cumuli become towering thunderheads.

From outside the storm area, air moves in over the sea surface to replace the air soaring upward in the thunderheads. The air begins swirling around the storm center, for the same reason that air swirls around a tornado's center.

As this air swirls in over the sea surface, it soaks up more and more water vapor. At the storm center, this new supply of water vapor gets pulled into the thunderhead updrafts, releasing still more energy as the water vapor condenses. This makes the updrafts rise faster, pulling in still larger amounts of air and water vapor from the storm's edges. And as the updrafts speed up, air swirls faster and faster around the storm center.

In another few days, the picture has changed. The storm has grown greatly in size and power. Now weather satellite photos show a swirl of clouds 400 miles wide. The swirl is shaped like a doughnut. At the center of this giant "doughnut" is a cloudless, ten-mile-wide hole. Through it, the blue waters of the ocean can be seen.

The storm clouds, moving with the swirling air, form a coil. It is this 100-mile-wide coil of clouds that the weather satellite "saw" at the beginning of this chapter.

This hole opened up as the winds swirling around the storm center neared hurricane speed— about 75 miles an hour. A simple experiment will show why this happens.

Suppose you try whirling a Yo-yo around your head. As it whirls, the Yo-yo seems to try to pull away from the hand holding its string. The faster you whirl it, the stronger this pull becomes.

In the same way, the winds of a forming hurricane tend to pull away from the center as the wind speed increases. When the winds move fast enough, the "hole" develops.

This hole is the mark of a full-fledged hurricane. It is called the eye of the hurricane. Within

A powerful hurricane some 200 miles east of the southern tip of Florida, as photographed from a weather satellite orbiting Earth. This hurricane, named Camille, caused heavy damage in Mississippi and Louisiana. For each year, hurricanes are given girls' names in alphabetical order of their appearance. For example, the first four hurricanes of 1973 were named Alice, Brenda, Christine, Delia. Camille was the third hurricane of 1969.

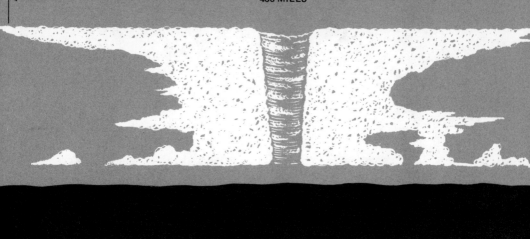

400 MILES

If you could slice the "doughnut" shape of a typical hurricane in half, this is what you would see. The "wall" of clouds around the central eye are whirled about by winds of over 75 miles an hour.

the eye, all is calm and peaceful. But in the cloud wall surrounding the eye, things are very different. There, howling winds swirl at speeds up to 150 miles an hour.

Although hurricane winds do not blow as fast as tornado winds, a hurricane is far more destructive. That's because tornado winds cover only a small area, usually less than a mile across. A hurricane's winds may cover an area 60 miles wide out from the center of the eye.

58

What's more, tornadoes rarely last as long as an hour, or travel more than 100 miles. However, a hurricane may rage for a week or more. In that time, it may travel tens of thousands of miles over sea and land.

At sea, hurricane winds whip up giant waves up to 20 feet high. Such waves can tear freighters and other oceangoing ships in half. Over land, hurricane winds can uproot trees, blow down telephone lines and power lines, and tear chimneys off rooftops. The air is filled with deadly flying fragments of brick, wood, and glass.

Much has been done to lessen danger from hurricanes. Weather satellite photos help meteorologists keep track of the storm's movements. The meteorologists can give hours of advance warning to people who may be in the path of a hurricane. Such warnings have saved hundreds of thousands of lives.

But, for some years now, a group of meteorologists have been taking the battle against hurricanes into the very heart of the storm itself. At Roosevelt Roads Naval Air Station, Puerto Rico, these scientists study photos of the hurricane we watched being born. The storm now has a name—Hurricane Debbie.

After studying the photos, the scientists

trudge out to the airstrip with their pilots. Over a period of hours, one plane after another takes off and heads for the cloud wall surrounding Debbie's eye. Miles above the storm-lashed ocean, the planes plunge into the cloud wall. Lightning flashes and thunder booms. But the pilots and scientists cannot hear the thunder above the shrieking winds. The planes shake. Their wings creak. Hail splatters against the cockpits like bullets.

While the pilots struggle to hold the planes steady, the scientists drop about 200 small can-shaped objects into the clouds. Each "can" sprays the clouds with thousands of tiny crystals of a chemical called silver iodide.

This is called seeding the clouds. After the seeding is done, each plane struggles out of the hurricane and returns to Puerto Rico. Scientists in other planes continue to fly in and out of Hurricane Debbie, watching for changes in the storm.

As we have seen, the "fuel" that drives a hurricane's winds is water vapor. Heat from condensing water vapor provides energy for the winds. When silver iodide crystals are dropped into the clouds, they cause more and more water vapor to condense and fall out of the clouds as rain. As

The flight path of an airplane "seeding" a hurricane. ➡

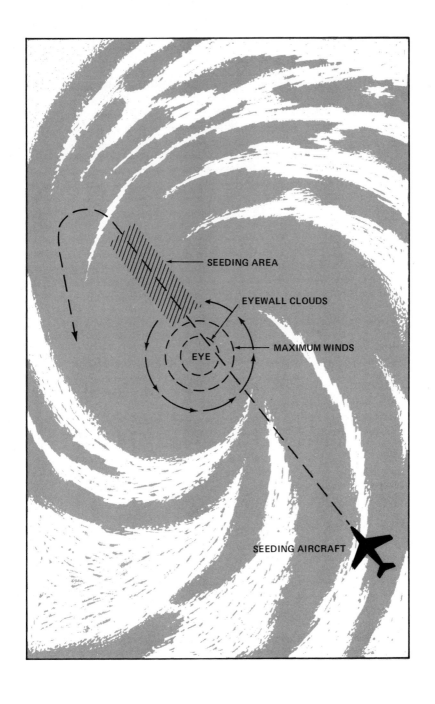

SEEDING AREA

EYEWALL CLOUDS

MAXIMUM WINDS

EYE

SEEDING AIRCRAFT

Debbie loses more "fuel," the scientists hope, her winds may slow down.

An hour after seeding, Debbie's peak winds drop from 112 miles an hour to 78 miles an hour. So the scientists go on experimenting with seeding. They may be on the way to taming hurricanes by giving them silver iodide linings!

However, many meteorologists point out that such seeding increases rainfall from a hurricane. In a sense, the seeding "squeezes" extra rain out of the storm in order to slow down its winds. Slower winds may do less damage, but heavier rains will bring more flooding. Hurricanes are part of the vast weather "machine" of the whole Earth itself. In trying to change one storm, man cannot always tell what changes he will bring about.

Dr. Alan T. Waterman, a former Director of the National Science Foundation, said this about man's problems in trying to change the weather: "We are here dealing with forces almost beyond our imagination and we must not forget that we could, without realizing it, set off a catastrophic reaction."

chapter **7**

The Biggest Storms

If you live in the continental United States, you've probably been through storms far bigger than any hurricane, and far more powerful. In fact, if you live anywhere in the Temperate Zones, such storms may be a common experience for you. There, a never-ending "war" rages as giant storms battle in the air.

The war is a struggle between two different kinds of air. Like some human wars, it is not won or lost. Like all human wars, it can cause great destruction. However, this warfare is necessary for life on this planet, and it often does great good.

In the Northern Hemisphere, the struggle is between two air masses: polar air and tropical air.

Polar air is cold and usually dry. It moves south-ward from the Arctic. On the other hand, tropical air is warm and moist. It moves northward from the equator.

Somewhere over the Temperate Zone, these

A map of temperature zones around the world. In general, weather in the frigid zones, around the North and South Poles, is always cold. Weather in the Tropics is always hot with just two seasons, a rainy season and a dry season. In the Temperate Zones, there are the four seasons most of us are familiar with: winter, spring, summer and fall, and the weather is changeable.

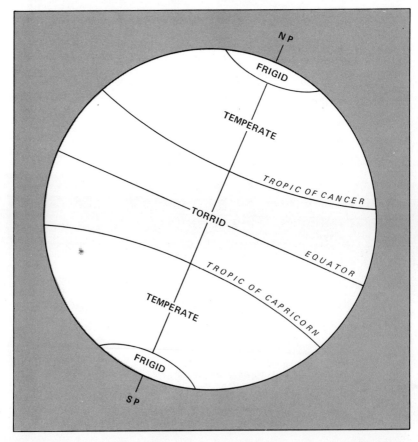

two air masses collide. But they do not mix. Instead, a boundary, or front, forms between them.

Sometimes the cold air mass advances, pushing the warm air mass ahead of it. This forms a cold front, which slants steeply upward. That's because the heavier, cold air pushes under the retreating warm air like a snowplow piling up snow.

In a cold front, a mass of cold air pushes under warmer air like a shovel piling up snow. Often, severe thunderstorms occur along such a front.

COLD AIR

WARM AIR

WARM AIR

COLD AIR

In a warm front, advancing warmer air replaces colder air. Since the warm air is lighter than the cold air it is replacing, the warm air tends to slope upward over the colder air. In a sense, this warmer air is "climbing a hill" of colder air.

Often, you can see a cold front as it approaches. In summer, it is most dramatic. Towering masses of cumulus and cumulonimbus clouds mark the edge of the front. It passes overhead, accompanied by drenching rain, lightning, and thunder. Behind the front, the sky clears rapidly. The air is dry, cool, and pleasant.

The weather is very different in the path of a warm front. Here the advancing warm air slopes

66

gently upward. Beneath it is a thin, long wedge of retreating cold air. This wedge may be a thousand miles long.

Imagine that you're a thousand miles away from the advancing edge of such a warm front. It will be several days before the warm front edge will reach you on the ground. But high overhead, clouds are already telling the story of the oncoming front.

Five or six miles up, the first traces of warm, moist air have reached the top of the cold air wedge. At that height, the air quickly cools to below freezing. Millions of tiny ice crystals form. The crystals are so tiny and so light that they float, making long, thin feathery wisps of cloud. These cirrus clouds usually give advance warnings of a warm front.

By next day, hazy, dull, flat stratus clouds blanket the sky. That makes it certain that a warm front is approaching. From now on, the clouds just keep getting lower and thicker.

At last, just ahead of the warm front's edge on the ground, it begins to drizzle. As the front passes you, the drizzle deepens into rain, which may last for hours. Behind the rain, the weather is hot, muggy, and hazy. The sky clears very slowly.

The long feathery wisps of cirrus clouds are made up of
tiny ice crystals. When these clouds begin appearing in
clear weather, watch the sky carefully. If cirrus clouds
thicken and the sky slowly becomes hazy during the day,
a large storm is probably on its way. You may get heavy
rain or snow and gusty winds in the next 12 to 24
hours....

As the storm passes overhead, low thick stratus clouds cover the sky. Some of the stratus clouds in this photograph are actually touching the ground. This forms fog. Fog is nothing more than a cloud at ground level.

These are typical weather patterns along a front. But often, when polar air collides with tropical air, a storm is born.

The diagrams and photos on pages 70 and 71 show how that happens. The photos, which were taken by a weather satellite, show such a storm being born and growing in the North Atlantic Ocean.

Compare the photos with the diagrams. The clouds tell the story of how the storm forms and grows. They show the same patterns as the diagrams.

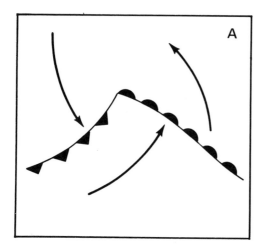 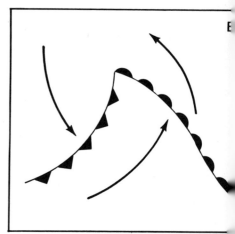

Drawings A and B show scientists' ideas about how a storm may form when tropical air and polar air collide. Meteorologists worked out these ideas some 50 years ago —long before weather satellites were put in orbit to actually photograph such storms as they form.

Photographs A and B, made by a weather satellite, show a storm being born. Notice how much like the drawings the photographs look. This is one kind of proof that the meteorologists' ideas were on the right track. In drawing A, a whirling motion of the warm and cold air begins. Line with rounded points is a warm front where light air is flowing "up-hill" over heavier cold air. Line with sharp points is a cold front where cold air is flowing "down-hill" under the warm air. At these fronts, clouds form. Photograph A shows how these clouds mark the edges of the fronts.

As the storm grows stronger, the air whirls faster. Because the cold air generally moves faster than the warm

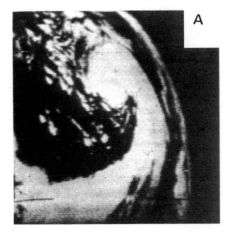

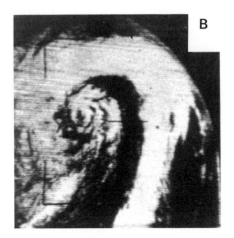

air, the cold front starts to "catch up" with the warm front. The sharp bend between the two fronts in drawing B shows this. Note the same sharp bend in the clouds in photograph B that mark the edges of the fronts.

Notice also the direction that the winds of the storm whirl in. It is the opposite direction to the way the hands of a clock move—counterclockwise. The winds of a storm whirl in this way because of the spinning of the Earth. However, south of the equator, storm winds whirl in the other direction—clockwise.

A simple experiment may help you see why this is so. Look down at the North Pole of a globe of the Earth. Turn the globe from west to east, in the way the real Earth turns. You will see the globe turning in a counterclockwise direction. Now—keeping the globe turning in the same direction—hold it over your head so that you are looking at the South Pole. You will see that the southern half of the globe is turning in a clockwise direction.

71

These storms are very different from hurricanes. They do not have eyes. They may form anywhere in the temperate zones, over land or over water. They may travel over half the world before they die out.

These storms are called cyclones. In everyday language, the word "cyclone" is often used to refer to a tornado. But meteorologists use cyclone to describe the storms that travel from west to east around the Temperate Zone.

Cyclones can be huge storms. One may be born in the South Pacific Ocean and take a week to cross to the United States. By the time it reaches the United States, it may be 2,000 miles wide.

That does not mean that it is raining or snowing over the entire 2,000 miles. The really stormy weather is in an area a few hundred miles wide around the center. However, the wind circulation around a large cyclone can affect the weather over two-thirds of the United States.

To see what can happen in a winter cyclone, let's track one that is 2,000 miles wide with its center around Chicago. For the area around the Great Lakes, that may mean heavy snow and high, icy winds.

Far off, the cyclone's western edge rests

against the Rocky Mountains. There the skies are clear, and the winds are gentle.

But the winds are blowing from the north, following the counterclockwise flow around the cyclone. The flow pulls in frigid air from Canada. Because of the cyclone, the mountain states are in the grip of a cold wave.

At first, the frigid air travels due south. Then it turns southeast and east. Cold and dry, it moves over the warm waters of the Gulf of Mexico. The air quickly picks up warmth and moisture from the Gulf. It turns northeast and north, flowing up the East Coast of the United States. In Florida and Georgia, the air is warm and muggy.

Further north, the air begins to cool. It becomes saturated. Water vapor condenses out of it. forming low, misty, drizzly stratus clouds. In some places, the clouds form at ground level, producing fog. Over the Northeastern United States, the air is chilly, damp, and foggy.

The long travels of this air around the cyclone show an important fact about these giant storms. They help keep the atmosphere well mixed. They move huge masses of polar air southward. This helps cool the tropics. They move huge masses of tropical air northward. This helps to warm the polar regions. Without cyclones, the polar regions would be much colder and the tropics much hotter.

What's more, by mixing polar and tropical air, the cyclones produce most of Earth's rainfall. Without cyclones, most of the United States, Europe, and Asia would soon be nothing but vast deserts. Cyclones are vital to life on Earth.

chapter 8

Scientific Guessing

The falling snow was so thick that the line of pines at the foot of the hill were hard to see. Her back to the fireplace, Margot watched the swirling flakes with glee. Snowstorms were the best part of winter, she thought. Tomorrow, she and her brother George could go sledding down the hill.

In the city, too, girls and boys were happy with the snow. There were parks and closed-off streets for their sleds and snowmen.

But parents were worried by the storm. The icy streets meant slippery walking and dangerous driving. In the country, deep snow drifts had to be shoveled away from front doors and driveways.

Meteorologists from New York City to Bangor, Maine, also worried as they watched the storm. They had made their forecasts yesterday. Many people depended on these forecasts in making their plans. But now, like everybody else, the meteorologists could only sit and watch. One weatherman who was watching this particular storm was Dr. Frank Field, of NBC-TV in New York City.

Before preparing his report, Dr. Field had studied the latest weather map in the New York office of the United States Weather Service. On the map, a gently curving line was drawn from Ohio through West Virginia, Virginia, North Carolina, and Florida.

The line, which had a series of toothlike points on it, marked the edge of a mass of cold air that was moving eastward across the United States. The line indicated a cold front. The teeth pointed in the direction that the cold air was moving.

To Dr. Field's trained eyes, the map was as clear as a picture. He could see the air of the cold front shoving along under the warmer, lighter air in its path. In South Carolina and Georgia, the cold front ran through the middle of two football-shaped ovals. These two ovals painted another part of the weather picture for Dr. Field. They marked the path of air that was beginning to swirl around the edge

Dr. Frank Field discusses problems of weather forecasting with the author.

of the cold front. Such a swirl, as we have seen, marks the beginning of a storm.

The young storm was not far from the Atlantic coast. That fact, Dr. Field realized, could have a great effect on the storm's future. The ocean acts as an enormous storehouse of heat energy. Its waters warm up slowly during spring and summer, and lose heat slowly during the winter months. Even now, in February, thought Dr. Field, the air temperatures just over the ocean off South Carolina would be 15 to 20 degrees warmer than air temperatures over the land.

If warm, moist air from the nearby ocean began flowing into the new storm, it would grow rapidly. The normal path for such a storm is northward up the coast. It could bring heavy snow to New York City and the Northeast. Or it could move out to sea.

But which would it be. The map showed what the weather was like now. Dr. Field had to decide what it would be like tomorrow.

He decided that the storm would bring heavy snow to the Northeast. That was his forecast.

The United States Weather Service forecast for the same period called for "snow beginning in the early morning hours, changing to rain. Rain ending in the early afternoon."

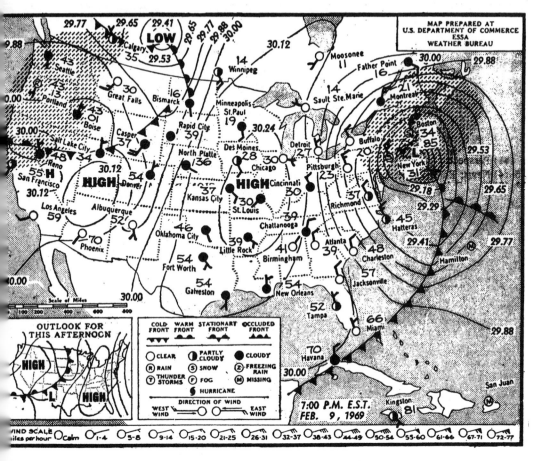

This is how the storm that brought 15 inches of snow to New York City looked on the weather map. Notice how this storm resembles the photos of a storm taken by weather satellite which appeared in the last chapter. The shaded area over the northeastern part of the United States shows where snow is falling.

What really happened? Fifteen inches of snow fell on the city.

"To some extent, I was lucky," says Dr. Field. "The many pieces of information that go into making a forecast are always changing. It's easy to slip up. For example: How fast was the storm going to move? Was it going to get stronger or weaker? What's the temperature going to be when the storm gets here? A degree below freezing, and you might have a bad snowstorm. A degree above, and you'd get nothing but rain.

"In this case, the Weather Service thought the storm would move faster than I did. They also thought the storm would be weaker and the temperature warmer.

"I happened to be right—this time. But I've made bad mistakes in the past, and the Weather Service has turned out to be right.

"We weathermen can usually warn you in time about hurricanes, tornadoes, and other natural disasters. But weather as a whole is too complicated to always predict accurately. Remember, we're scientific guessers—not magicians."

You can be a scientific guesser, too. You can see exactly what the local weather is like from your own backyard or your own window. What story do the clouds tell?

Was the sky filled with feathery cirrus clouds this morning? Have the clouds slowly become thicker and more milky-looking? Then your forecast might be: "Rain or snow (depending on how warm or cold it is) tomorrow."

Or perhaps you can see a line of thunderheads moving in your direction from the north or northwest. Then your forecast might be: "Heavy rain accompanied by lightning and thunder. Clearing and colder in a few hours."

Like Columbus, you can learn a lot about your local weather—just by watching the sky.

Safety Rules

(These safety rules are adapted from official bulletins of the United States Weather Bureau.)

Thunderstorms

1. When cumulus clouds start billowing up and getting dark, you are probably in for a thunderstorm. Check the radio for the latest forecast.

2. Keep calm. Thunderstorms don't usually last more than half an hour. Be careful, but don't be afraid.

3. Know what the storm is doing. A sudden rise in wind speed and a sharp drop in temperature mean that the storm is about to break. Heavy rain, hail, lightning and sometimes tornadoes may follow. (See safety rules for tornadoes.)

4. Lightning is the thunderstorm's worst killer. Stay indoors while the storm is overhead. If you live in the city or in a modern building of steel construction, you are safe from lightning indoors. If you live in the country, stay away from indoor wires during the storm. Avoid touching metal surfaces, such as bathtubs, sinks, radiators, furnaces, washing machines, dryers and dishwashers. A bolt may strike the wiring outside and leap from metal surface to metal surface on its path to the ground. Also, don't handle plug-in electrical devices. Don't use the telephone, except in an emergency.

5. If you're caught outdoors, DON'T seek shelter under a lone tree or a beach umbrella. Stay a safe distance away from any tall, isolated object. About twice the height of the object is a safe distance.

6. Don't swim or fish. If lightning strikes the water, it can charge large areas of it with deadly amounts of electricity. A fishing line will carry this charge directly to your body. If you're in a boat, head for shore immediately. Once docked, get away from the shore area.

7. Don't ride a bicycle, scooter, or horse.

8. If you are in a car that has been struck by lightning, you will be perfectly safe so long as you stay in the car. But since the car's tires are rubber, electricity cannot easily flow to the ground from the steel frame of the car. So the frame may hold a deadly charge for some time after the strike. If you step from the car with one foot in the car and the other on the ground, this charge will pass into the ground through you. To be safe, a metal object should be used to connect frame to ground before anyone leaves the car. When this is done, the charge will drain from the frame instantly.

Winter Storms

1. If you live in an area where big winter storms are common, you and your parents should prepare for storm safety before winter sets in. This includes stocking a good supply of food that does not need to be cooked or refrigerated, in case of power failure.

2. If you and your family are caught in your car during a bad snowstorm in open country, stay in the car. You can lose your way easily in blowing and drifting snow. Keep a car window partly open opposite the windy side. Exercise by clapping your hands and moving arms and legs from time to time. Put some real effort into these motions. Don't stay in one position for long.

Tornadoes

1. Listen regularly to radio or TV weather reports during the tornado season. A broadcast of a <u>tornado watch</u> means that conditions are ripe for a tornado to form. If a tornado watch is announced, stay tuned. A storm may approach suddenly, even if the sky is blue. Look for dark, threatening clouds approaching. There may not be time for a <u>tornado warning</u> broadcast. Stay alert for sudden heavy rain and hail or a funnel-shaped cloud. Listen for a sudden increase in wind noise. When in doubt, take cover (see below).

2. A tornado warning means that a tornado has actually been sighted or picked up by radar. If

it is nearby, seek shelter immediately. A storm cellar is the best shelter. STAY AWAY FROM ALL WINDOWS.

3. In homes, a storm cellar offers the best protection. If you don't have a storm cellar, seek shelter in your basement, under heavy sturdy furniture. If you have no basement, take cover in the center part of the house on the lowest floor in a small room, such as a closet or under sturdy furniture. Keep some windows open, but don't go near them. In a basement, the safest spot is the corner nearest the approaching storm.

4. In open country, if there is no shelter nearby, lie down in the nearest hole, such as a ditch or a ravine, and hold your arms over your head to protect it from falling objects.

Hurricanes

1. A hurricane watch broadcast means there is a hurricane some distance away. It is not yet known whether it is likely that the storm will strike your area.

2. A <u>hurricane warning</u> means the hurricane is very likely to hit your area. You and your parents should make sure you have a good supply of food and water. The food should need no cooking or refrigeration. You should also have a flashlight, candles, and a battery-operated radio.

3. Loose objects, such as tools and trash barrels, should be put away. Otherwise, high winds may turn them into deadly missiles.

4. Leave some windows open on the side of the house opposite from the approaching storm. To tell what direction the storm is approaching from, face into the wind. Your right side will now be turned toward the storm.

Glossary

Air Mass–A large body of air, all of about the same temperature and containing the same amount of water vapor.

Atmosphere–The envelope of gases that surrounds a world.

Cold Front–The boundary formed when a cold air mass advances, pushing a warm air mass ahead of it.

Condenses–Changes from a gas to a liquid.

Conductor–Anything through which electricity flows easily.

Cyclones–The large storms which travel from west to east around the Temperate Zone, produced by the collision of Polar and Tropical air.

Downdraft–A falling column of cool air. It is the opposite of updraft.

Electrons–The negative charges which swirl around the nucleus of an atom.

Evaporate–Turn from liquid into a gas.

Hurricane Warning–The alert issued by the weather bureau when a hurricane is heading into a populated area.

Hurricane Watch–An alert that a hurricane may strike a populated area.

Meteorologists–Scientists who study the weather.

Protons–The positive charges contained in the nucleus of an atom.

Tornado Warning–An alert issued as soon as a tornado is sighted.

Tornado Watch–An alert isued when conditions are ripe for a tornado.

Troposphere–The lower, stormy part of the atmosphere.

Updraft–A column of warm air which rises because warm air is lighter than surrounding cold air.

Warm Front–The boundary formed when a warm air mass advances and pushes a cold air mass ahead of it.

Water Vapor–Water in the form of an invisible gas.

Index

Air
  cold front, 65-66, 76
  cooling, 27, 31, 50
  downdraft, 27
  in motion, 24
  in outer space, 24
  masses, 63, 65, 76
  moisture, 51, 53, 54, 55
  Polar, 63, 64, 69, 73-74
  saturation, 27
  swirling, 55, 56, 76-77
  temperature, 24
  Tropical, 63, 64, 69, 73-74
  updraft, 21, 24, 36, 27, 52,
    54, 55
  warm ceiling, 55
  warm front, 66-67
Arctic Ocean, 64

Atlantic Ocean, 9, 54,
  69-71, 78
  as energy source, 78
Atmosphere, 24
  temperatures of, 24
Atoms, 37-38

Canada, 50, 73
Caribbean Sea, 9, 10, 54
  weather of, 9-14
Chicago, 72
Cirrus clouds, 67, 81
Clouds
  coils, 56
  formation of, 21, 24
  electrical charges, 38-42
  "seeding" clouds, 60-62
  shape of, 16, 20, 21

signs of weather, 16

what clouds are, 17-25

Cold wave, 73

Columbus, Christoper, 9-16,
  54, 81

Cumulus clouds, 21, 24,
  26, 55

explosion of, 25, 26-35

Cumulonimbus clouds, 66

Cyclones, 63-74

path of, 72, 73

producer of rainfall, 74

war on air masses, 63-67

width of, 72

Electricity

charges, positive and
  negative, 36-38

conductor of, 42

friction, 37, 38

in thunderstorm, 38

Electrons, 38, 40

friction of, 38, 40

Energy, release of, 55

Equator, 54, 64

Faraday, Michael, 42

Faraday's cage, 42

Field, Dr. Frank, 76-80

Florida, 73

Fog, 73

Franklin, Benjamin, 43

Georgia, 73

Great Lakes, 72

Great Western Plains,
  50, 52, 53

Gulf of Mexico, 50, 52, 53, 73

Hail, 52, 60

Hispaniola, (See Santa
  Domingo)

Hurricanes, 10, 11, 14, 24,
  56-62

damage on land, 59

doughnut shape, 56

effect on sea, 59, 60

eye of, 56, 58

extent of, 58-59

formation of, 54, 56

length of, 59

safety in, 87

"seeding," 60-62

signs of, 14
speed of, 56, 58
taming, 59-62
time of year, 54
winds, 58
Hurricane Debbie, 59-60, 62
Hurricane Warning, 14, 53, 59
Hurricane Watch, 53

Ice Crystals, 31, 37, 67

Keller, Will, 44, 45-58

Lightning, 35, 36-43, 66, 81
  bolts, 42
  conductor, 42
  heat of, 43
  injury from, 36
  in tornado, 48
  safety, indoors, 84
  safety, outdoors, 84
  speed of, 42
  what lightning is, 36-37

Meteorologist, 21, 59, 60,
  62, 72, 76
  Dr. Frank Field, 76-80

Northern Hemisphere, 63

Pacific Ocean, 72
Protons, 37-38, 40
Puerto Rico, 54, 59, 60

Rain, 35, 60, 62, 66, 67,
  74, 78, 81
Rocky Mountains, 73
Roosevelt Roads Naval Air
  Station, 59

Safety Rules
  in Hurricanes, 87
  in Thunderstorms, 83-85
  in Tornadoes, 86-87
  in Winter (snow)
    storms, 85
San Salvador, Island of, 9
Santa Domingo, 10, 14
Shock Wave, 43
Silver Iodide, 60, 62
SKYWARN, 53
Snow, 31, 37, 72, 74, 78, 80
  safety in, 84
Spain, 9, 10, 11, 14

Storms, 10, 11, 14, 24
  in United States, 14-15
  winter, 16
Stratus clouds, 67, 73
Sun, 21, 26

Temperate Zone, 63, 64, 72
Thunder
  cause of, 43
  sound of, 43, 60, 66
Thunderhead, 31, 55, 81
Thunderstorm, 10, 24, 31, 35,
  37, 38, 41, 44, 52, 53
  electrical charges in, **38-42**
  safety in, 84
Tornadoes, 16, 24, 44-53
  air pressure, 49-50
  extent of, 16, 59
  funnel, 46-47, 49, 55
  human injury, 48, 53
  number, in U.S., 50
  property damage, 16,
    48-49, 50
  protection against, 44
  safety in, 86-87
  SKYWARN, 53
  wind speed, 48-49, 58
Tornado Alley, 50, 53

Tornado Cellar, 44-45
Tornado Warning, 53
Tornado Watch, 53
Troposphere, 25, 31

U.S. Weather Service, 76,
  78, 80

Waterman, Dr. Alan T., 62
Water Vapor, 20, 21
  condensation, 20, 21, 27,
    52, 55, 60, 73
  evaporation, 26, 27
  heat energy, stored, 20,
    55, 60
  heating and cooling, 52,
    54, 55
Weather
  forecasting, 75-81
  in the Caribbean, 9-14
  in space, 24
Weather Map, 76, 79
Weather Satellites, 14, 54,
  56, 59
Wind, 9, 10, 14, 31, 37, 72
  in cyclone, 72-73
  in hurricane, 56-58, 60
  swirling, 48, 52, 53-55, 56